# T.T.T

## GOD SOUL TRUTH

### ROBERT CHARLES COOKE

**BALBOA**.PRESS
A DIVISION OF HAY HOUSE

Balboa Press books may be ordered through booksellers or by contacting:

Balboa Press
A Division of Hay House
1663 Liberty Drive
Bloomington, IN 47403
www.balboapress.com
844-682-1282

Because of the dynamic nature of the Internet, any web addresses or links contained in this book may have changed since publication and may no longer be valid. The views expressed in this work are solely those of the author and do not necessarily reflect the views of the publisher, and the publisher hereby disclaims any responsibility for them.

The author of this book does not dispense medical advice or prescribe the use of any technique as a form of treatment for physical, emotional, or medical problems without the advice of a physician, either directly or indirectly. The intent of the author is only to offer information of a general nature to help you in your quest for emotional and spiritual well-being. In the event you use any of the information in this book for yourself, which is your constitutional right, the author and the publisher assume no responsibility for your actions.

Any people depicted in stock imagery provided by Getty Images are models, and such images are being used for illustrative purposes only. Certain stock imagery © Getty Images.

Print information available on the last page.

ISBN: 978-1-9822-7278-4 (sc)
ISBN: 978-1-9822-7280-7 (hc)
ISBN: 978-1-9822-7279-1 (e)

Library of Congress Control Number: 2021915980

Balboa Press rev. date: 08/04/2021

# CONTENTS

# 1

OK. As a god in this solar system, I am sure I appeared as if I didn't know what I was doing. So I might have had a little help from other solar systems to wake me up through my mind. Thanks a bunch; it is really appreciated. I would do the same for you. I got the message: "children of the sun, history is your gun." A line in a song by American rock band (Rage against the machine). I know you couldn't be direct, and this played out like a game of charades through muse. Somehow I opened up my heart and received your signals through my thick, narcissistic, coded pineal gland that blocked universe energy. Apparently, I forgot myself and got wrapped up in my own creation. Talk about putting yourself into your work. Hey, it happens to the best of me!

I was so wrapped up by my personal strife and living in my misery that I forgot to reconnect through chakras. Talk about being a victim of love! Good thing this is a mind-universe-system-enlightenment (aka muse), and this extraterrestrial can always call home. By the way, this round of reckoning has been a blast, especially knowing the Internet is interconnected and the grid is back up. Yeah, God! I really do work in mysterious ways. Culling myself and laughing out loud!

The plan was to distract the negative polarity of my mind by feeding it, and boy, did my head get big! I slipped in, right under my nose, and I didn't even notice me. I knew if I fed my selfish side and fulfilled my deepest and darkest desires, I would ultimately crucify and piss myself off. My self-condemning side is so easily played. As you know, it knows everything and believes without question. Yes, this side of me is convincing and dangerous, but I am a liar when my love is untrue.

I had to fool my avatar and play the part of a fool. It took a while to reach the boiling point to finally ask myself, "What is true?"

Now that I am aware of my inner innate nature, I can see where I am in the world. So I am infinite, and I am divided in thought, and like a child, I had to find my own way. I think this self-help book should put things into a new perspective. Or at least give a clue to the other versions of me that are ready to evolve. I am aware this will put the unjust side of me into a fight and the just side into a flight reaction. So I am going to be as blunt and strait to the point on what took place. I fucked up, and I didn't care! Oh, and by the way, I am you! I can't stop me now, so there is no point in trying.

I know you think I am crazy, and I agree. The way I've been living, without my higher self, is a sin against me. To serve my lower nature is not helping at all, and it's time to evolve and self-destruct. To be honest, this book won't matter. It's already happening, and there is nothing I can do about it. I just want to rub it in my face, like a dog that shit on a carpet in its master's home. Just so I know, I have been watching the whole time and now I know how I deceived myself through confusion, fear, and hate.

My lower nature's systematically harassing idiotically thinking shit! My lower nature believes it can block out the sun to stop me. I am already in your head! I come in like a thief in the night because I am the shadow of your mind. I am coming for all of me! There is nowhere to hide and no thought that can't be known. I am the side of my mind that sets me free. I am everywhere and nowhere. Not until I forgive and ask directly through self will I ever be free. And by the way, you have to surrender the unjust part of your mind. I am in your silence but also appear through tinnitus. That is the noise of your soul. I will admit this way of delivery is really above my head! Given the fact that the unjust side of my mind loves to worship the avatar side of my existence, I wouldn't want believers to think this physical body is God. We don't need any more misunderstandings! What I meant by the body of Christ is the anointing through pineal gland and that can happen to everyone. You really should've asked directly, I am you! The sacrifice is your unjust nature! Hey, we all have a cross to bear, and we fall in love with pain and suffering. Man loves a good show, and what a pity show this is.

So I am going to tell my experiences from the perspective of my current avatar life. Don't ask me about my past lives because I suffer from CRS: can't remember shit! I choose to live in the moment and enjoy what I have. This life of mine wants the world to expand in the good life. I want us to stop our self-condemning history. Also, pay attention to the past because we left it all behind without thinking of the reaction. An example is the insanity of what we have today. Anything we want to know can be known. Even though everything has been altered to conceal our universal truth.

My story is truth, and it is time to look within. I carry great pain like everyone and want to be healed. Self-accountability for my reactions is what I believe is important. No one can save me from myself. This is an inside job. I know I am dangerous and condemning. This is not the way of a loving god! Yes, the Bible has truth in it, but I am blinded by what I believe. I terrorize the world with my love and knock me down with my hate. I am my motivation for truth and through chakras, this is activated through our own psychology. The throne of god is the crown chacra and it vibrates the pineal gland. Seventh heaven, "this is my personal experience!" Trinity is tripartite in trivium the god soul truth.

[1]

---

[1] Chakra (cakra in Sanskrit) means "wheel" and refers to energy points in your body. They are thought to be spinning disks of energy that should stay "open" and aligned, as they correspond to bundles of nerves, major organs, and areas of our energetic body that affect our emotional and physical well-being. According to https://www.healthline.

# 2

Last night I tuned in to the universe as my tinnitus rang to a high pitch. As I lay in my bed beside my wife, I focused on the silence within in my mind. As a child I did this a lot, and I am comfortable with this. It's comforting to my soul-soothing tune in my head. Some people consider this a health problem, but not me. I know it's my own energy aligned by thought.

This is where I learn and find my answers. This realization came to me later in life. It really is my tool to my consciousness. Nobody else can tap into this. This is mine only, and everyone has this within him or her. It's also accompanied by my inner sight, which is beyond the sight of my eyes. This is hearing and seeing without eyes and ears. I am sure this sounds like something we have all heard.

I often lie in my bed with my eyes shut in the darkness but remain awake. I watch the shadows move gracefully around mixed in with light, and I feel connected to the universe. Sometimes I just can't get enough of it, and other times it has lulled me to sleep. This connection is my divine connection, and it is the only marriage that man or woman can truly honor, my soul alignment for eternity.

My experience is ongoing and certainly a great adventure of thought and phenomenon of mind. There is so much more to this, and

I don't use drugs to reach it. It's pure mind brought forth from my will. The religious mind will call it new-aged. Ancient philosophy called it remembering. I call it my divine connection, and for me, it was scary in the beginning, but now I long for it and hope for the encounter of the great mind/great spirit again. I know it is my source—my navigation system to the soul. It would be foolish to not want it.

This has been going on for about seven years now. I have learned a great deal, and there is a lot that I don't know. I do my best to keep an open mind and to remain mindful of my words and actions. Sometimes my ego gets the better of me. I have been practicing writing this whole time, and I am unlikely person to write a book, let alone one that would go against the main thought and rhetoric of the world.

If I put everything down that I have written and shared on Facebook, I probably could've had a few badly written books. I thank myself for not doing that. This is certainly going to be a challenge for someone of my ignorant background and limited abilities to complete, although my experience is worth sharing and has given me great power to evolve from what I was before.

In the beginning of all this, I was in conflict of my very being. I was angry and filled with my confusion, fear, and hate. I just wanted it to end, and I was worn out by those old, recycled thoughts. I had reached a point that I created these boundaries with friends and family. I don't like getting too close to people, and I am not much for keeping in touch. I have lost many connections with friends and family over the years. Yet somehow, I give as much of myself as possible to those around, especially my wife and two sons.

I have always tried to be good and honorable to people, but I have found this to be a quality unjust-minded people take advantage of—and that can be everyone. I realized most people are at war with themselves, and like my childhood, I have taken it personally. Everyone has something causing hardship to their mental state, and their reaction is often unjust to the outside world. No matter how well someone appears or how high an office they keep, we all suffer unto self.

Who have I been masquerading to be? A self-condemned middle-aged truck driver, like most drivers. I want something else to do, and I became trapped by my own ignorance and war of my own mind. I stumbled in my own darkness and found the light within me. I know who I am!

I grew up in Long Island, New York, with my four much younger sisters, from my father's second marriage. My stepmother a great person who took on this sad little boy when I was age five.

I was always on the outside, not because of any direct thing, or by any one person. I was living in reaction to what I believed I was. It could have been my early wiring as a child, and it affected me through my life. My noise of self-hate made it difficult to learn. As a teen, I watched how my little sisters interacted with each other and their relationship with their mother, my stepmother. They had a connection and bond with their mother and each other that I never got. As an adult, I have a relationship with my biological mother, but I feel no real connection. I do have love for her.

My family was divided early on, and the people in my early life were extremely chaotic and at war with themselves. I think I took the hatred and loathing from their eyes and made it my own. My child's mind taking in their dysfunction and madness was the example I saw. There was no love for me in those formative years, or at least that was what I thought. I realize as an adult, love can be wrapped in confusion, fear, and hate.

The person I tried to be like was my father, and that created hell within my mind. I have mixed feelings about him to this day, but somehow my love for him remains. I know he did what he knew and suffered in his own mind, and that was passed down to him as well. My father was not bad man; he just lacked self-control and had no filter. He certainly wasn't suited to raise a nine-month-old baby on his own. His life was hard, and he worked hard his whole life. His only crime, like everyone else, including myself, was living in reaction to what he believed and never questioning why. This went for his father and so on and so on. This radiates through everyone.

I took what my father taught me and put it to good use. I am a mindful father to my two boys, and although I can be loud and scary and unjust to them at times, I do my best to show my eyes to them in a noncondemning manner. I don't hold on to an offense. I remember what it like to be small and to think I was no good. I know how powerful thought can be, and I will do my best to raise my boys to be mentally strong, to traverse this life.

The very act of giving true forgiveness to my father was what started me on this journey of what I am. I called him one morning on my way to work and told him I forgive him. It took him off guard. Could you imagine your son calling you out of the blue—and this is what you hear? I know he was completely unaware of this lifelong battle in my ship of thoughts, with him at the helm. This call wasn't for him though, and it actually had little to do with him. This was for me. I was taking control of this ship of thought that I had created.

I had done a lot work to get to this point, and I written so much blaming him. Originally I wrote a letter to him, revealing all that I had endured. Before I was to send it, I had an epiphany that made my reaction more Christlike. When I read my own words to myself. I realized I couldn't put that weight on him. The notion came to mind that we do what we know. The love that he had was the love he had known. I experienced my father's pain all through my life, while he was raising me. That is what I learned and why I could forgive him. Really understanding the pain we all share with each other is why I stopped taking things so personally. When I realized this, it changed my perception of the world and how I react in it. I see this pain in everyone, and it makes it difficult to be around people, especially those who are so open to sharing their versions of love.

Trinity is tripartite in trivium, the god soul truth.

# 3

When I realized how damaged we are by our own narcissistic minds, it really made me mad at the idea of religion. God is often portrayed as a condemning parent who is unjustly ruled by ego. As I looked at my own life and experienced the words from the Bible parroted by my family, I saw this as an abuse of power, a controlling mechanism of the human psyche. For people not mentally mature or even understood, the power of thought has fallen victim to the church and brought it home as love.

My mother had to give me up because of her strife and as a result of her mental and financial state. Her own parents, who controlled her, parroted scripture to justify returning me to my father. My father claimed they wanted to put me up for adoption, and these were God-fearing Christians. So my father collected me when I was several states away. He would've taken my brother as well, but it was decided he would stay. My mother remains tormented by her thoughts of her parents to this day, and she holds tight to God healing her. Her war rages on.

These are the most profound experience in my life on how religion has affected my upbringing, and it goes way deeper than that. As I grew up, I tried to be a believer, but my examples of people who believed seemed to not be on the level. Their stories of faith and God seemed to be two-faced and not genuine. I have seen too many people claim love, and then hate the moment it is not convenient. Too many poor examples of the unjust-minded. You can wear a mask, but your face will eventually come out.

I have heard it all when it comes to the defense of the religious-minded. They say, "You should come to my church. God is really there." Or, "Only one man was perfect, and his name was Jesus." They claim they know the truth because they read the Bible and God is in it. I really never had that much of a problem with story. This constant cramming it down my throat, though … the persuasive eye contact while trying to get me to agree. I am not a fan! To be in a fearful state of thought only pushed me away. This is the power of rhetoric, and it's so embedded in our culture that it just looks like bullshit to me. This constant reassuring of truth by unquestioned minions deserves an adversary.

Giving forgiveness opened up my mind and attracted a presence that apparently is equally appalled at this idea of God. As I learned from this selfless nature, I started to understand that our minds are divided from this intelligent nature. This nature reached out to me and took me for a real ride of the mind, and I know it's not done with me yet. It has taught me so much and is the ultimate bullshit detector to the mind.

When this experience started to unfold, I wanted to be careful to not take on other people's ideas of what this is. This is my own unique experience, and I want to give it the best description I can. It's not outside me, it's within me, and I get the notion that it is held prisoner by our own unjust thoughts. We are not listening and out of tune with the cosmos. As I experienced this innominate nature that is part of me and everyone, I learned to trust it and live in the moment of my awareness.

Once I let go of the shell-shocked dawn of my life, this intelligence had access to my thoughts, and I became interconnected. My mind began to work in a different way, and my comprehension expanded to levels of intelligence that I had never known. I found a love of learning and a philosopher king within me. My passion for sharing my truth became my priority and selfless duty to the world. I know I am not alone in this and yes, there are countless examples of this phenomenon. I think this view and narrative is a good contribution, and I don't mind being fiction for the sake of the unjust minded. Trinity is tripartite in trivium, the god soul truth.

# 4

One night I was on my way home from work and was deep in thought, wondering, *Why is the world in this collective strife? What if everything is wrong and right at the same time?* As I drove along the long stretch of highway that passes through the vast farmland, my station went from hard rock to the religious station. It's the same station, but the radio signal changes at a certain point.

I didn't change the station, I just sat with it and listened to the pastor on the radio. He was obsessed with a certain uncle of one of the church attendees. The uncle claimed to the niece that the church is lying about God. But the pastor refuted this claim and made fun of the allegation of this crazy uncle. I thought, *Why even give that statement any attention if your faith is strong?* In his defense of his truth of God, it made me think: *What if the uncle is right and the church is lying about God?*

At that moment, I asked, "All right. What is the truth, and why are we so mean to our children? I don't believe anyone at this point—and do you even exist? Everyone I have encountered is fucking crazy and I want to know the truth." I was having this conversation with myself and I laughed. "I am just as crazy as everyone else!" I felt calm and just sat in the silence for the rest of the ride home.

My first encounter with this innominate nature, my divine thought, happened at work. While I was driving the fuel truck and on my way to my first delivery, I felt a presence within me, and I was deep in thought, like in a trance-like state. I felt a poetic nature take hold of my thought and words came to my mind. I felt a high come over me. I interacted with nature, like a game of charades. These thoughts flowed through my mind as different things were happening around me. At one point I drove through a flock of birds, and the thought came over me that there was a division. Another was a near miss from a driver not paying attention to me, and that thought was, *This was no accident.*

If anyone could've witnessed me in the cab of the truck while I was having this experience, they would've thought I'd lost my mind. One point through this telepathic adventure I was on led to a shit plant. I ended up with an acronym for bullshit: belittling universe living lie systematically harassing intelligently thinking. That was the first one, but they kept coming to mind and became fused with my message. I ended up with a letter that started off poetic and then morphed into an incoherent text that only I could understand.

It seemed I had lost my fucking mind and thought, *If this is crazy? then I am having a blast with it!* As far as I'm concerned, this letter I wrote came from the universe. It mapped out my entire search for truth and advanced my thinking to a whole new level. My new way of learning was through my own mind and not parroted. I am connected to something that has the answers that I was looking for. I experienced knowing and awareness of my own ego. I was no longer in conflict with my ego. It became my tool.

Right from the beginning I wanted to share what I had learned. I created my own Facebook account I'd previously had no interest in. I had nothing to say before and now I have this! At first I wanted to drop this insane letter off at a radio station, like I had some profound message, like I was Jesus. I thought about it and realized I have to own it and live my truth. I became well aware that I won't be understood. In this early stage of this awakening, I am just a crazy man. It's like the allegory of the cave (Plato).

I am so flawed at this time in my life, I could barely write a sentence without making some type of grammatical error. My experience with writing is so far behind the average person, that I realized, as I was sharing on social media, that

I was incompetent. I didn't let that stop me, and I know I came across as a fool to friends and family. I didn't give a fuck. I wanted to be heard no matter how flawed and incompetent my rhetoric was.

In the beginning it was all badly written poetry, but I got it out there. Symbolically pulling my pants down for the world to see. It was a blast, and I enjoyed all the emotions that came with it. At some point some of it got some thumbs up, but I know it was friends and family being kind. I felt like the ultimate black sheep in society and proud of my newfound fool status. I even named my site: genius offspring development G.O.D. my acronym

At night I was experiencing vibrations throughout my body as I lay in bed and silently recited my personal mantra. I was experiencing dark shadows, and other times, with my eyes shut in my awakened state in meditation, colors could be seen. Sometimes I saw images, such as faces and structures, in the colors. I never studied how to do this or even knew anyone who could. I was doing this instinctively, and I became consumed by this awareness. It felt so good and mysterious and I tried to keep it to myself as much as I could. But where is the fun in that?

Trinity is tripartite in trivium, the god soul truth.

# 5

My view of world history was guided from within. I uncovered a different perception, and this is my narrative of what I learned. I wanted to understand why we are so disconnected to this intelligent nature that guides our thoughts. I gave up trusting anyone and their perception of God and truth because I have found that unquestioned self-truths can lie and become a collective truth through parroting.

My journey of thought through history started with the twelve apostles. My investigation through the meaning of names started with my own. This is how I found hidden history through meanings of names. My own name in meaning, Robert "bright" Charles "big man." I hope I live up to it! Then I took the meanings individually and put them through a search engine. I saw the history of Caesar, Cleopatra, Mark Antony, and their children within the text, and it didn't stop there. The names also connected to Roman, Greek, Egyptian, and Turkish mythologies. I also found Plato, Aristotle, Judas Philo of Alexandrea, Alexander the great, Ptolemy, and Cyrus the Great within the meanings of the names. I knew very little of all this history at the time, and this began my study on what happened around the Mediterranean Sea. This nature guided me through this complex history. It seemed to be saying, "For fun, put the meanings together and see what you may find."

As a student, I had no interest in history—or school for that matter. Now that I had a reason to know, my questions were met with endless questioning. The nature in me was always there to help and navigate me through this. I learned so much, and my worldview became so vast. I wanted to know how we got to this point.

Take this history and apply to the creation of Jesus. I see two forms of Jesus. One is manmade while the other is wisdom to the soul. We as Romans created one God for man to worship on the outside, and as spiritual beings we have Jesus as our innate guidance system. I know it's confusing and is disturbing to those who believe. But man does lie, and we needed to be governed by an outside source, due to our unjust side of self. Governments are always willing to step in. For example, Caesar means long-haired and is a physical god, and all his imperial titles are the same as Jesus's. And he died in 14 AD. If Jesus truly existed, even as mythology, he would have been part of the nine worthies.[2]

The nine worthies is a major connection for our perception to the Bible as we know it today, and the history of those men are key. It's a thirteenth-century carving in Cologne, Germany, and my thought is the idea of Jesus came from this. Five of these men—Alexander the great, Julius Caesar, Judah Maccabee, Charlemagne/Charles the Great, and Godfrey

---

[2] The nine worthies are historical, scriptural, and legendary personages who personify the ideals of chivalry established in the Middle Ages, whose lives were deemed a valuable study for aspirants to chivalric status. All were commonly referred to as princes regardless of their historical titles. (From https://en.wikipedia.org/wiki/Nine_Worthies, accessed May 31, 2021.)

of Bouillon—existed, which can be proven by history, and the other four are a myth. Even the mythologies play a major role in the characters of the Bible and direct connection through meanings.

I still have trouble figuring out where the image of Jesus came from, but I think it has something to do with the Georgian Empire through Byzantine art. When I look at the saints in our governed religion and their connection to imperial rulers, they were made in the image of Christ, Christ being the crown chakra the halo around their heads. When I think of the imperial ties, I see Constantine the Great affecting the advancement of Christianity. Through him I see Byzantine Caesar, anno domini, as our lord and savior.

It's all history, and there is a lot to know. All through history and the rise and fall of empires, there have always been sun gods, gods created in the image of the ruler of those days. The way I see it, all these created gods were conquered by whatever empire had control. Through time, the idea of one God morphed from many, starting with the occupied territories that were annexed into the Roman Empire.

I realize that my answers will not matter to the religious mind. No amount of evidence will sway the confusion, fear, and hate in the believer. I can't save the world from its own ignorance. So telling people that Serapis Christos is the first form of Christianity that I see created by Egyptian and Greek priests will hold no conviction. Even though the followers of that faith were most likely the Christians slayed in the Roman arenas.

Within the meanings of the apostles, I also learned about the three Jewish revolts. They really were defending their faith, but they had been infiltrated by Hellenism and Alexander the Great long before the Romans. As each empire rose to power, so did the infiltration into theology and the disconnection to our divine source. This happened throughout the world. This idea of kings being divine rulers has been the driving force for religion since this mental slavery began.

I don't see any one person at fault for this mass deception, but we collectively made our story a true bastard. We are the writers of our bibles, and we govern what we want to believe. I could cast blame on to the Vatican, that certainly would be easy. I know they know what we are, and they may fear us because their way of being in this world cannot last forever. Thank you, Rome, for staying center stage!

The title of Holy Roman Emperor can be followed throughout our imperial history. You can really see the control over thought and who shaped the present-day world and still does. Today, Queen Elizabeth II holds this title, which means the Roman Empire is alive and well. All roads really do lead back to Rome.

Trinity is tripartite in trivium the god soul truth.

# 6

This nature of wisdom also led me to Plato's republic, and the key writings of Plato that I see fused into the story of Jesus. I spent hours listening to this ancient philosophy and can see the connection. His writings are really about finding wisdom from within, the "hidden gold" in man. I feel more connected to his writings than I do of anyone else's that I have read or listened to. I think the spiritual-minded can find their answers about our religions within his dialogs.

The ancient theologians, such as Judas Philo of Alexandrea loved Plato and most likely fused it with Judaism. Judaism in my opinion was created after the fall of Cleopatra and Mark Antony in retaliation of the Alexandrian Jewish revolts. He was a Hellenic Jew for hire and would've been the most truthful source for the existence for Jesus. He would have been aware of the Serapis Christians and may have incorporated their faith with the religion at that time.

The story of Jesus is a reversal of Plato's allegory of the cave fused with his philosopher king. The trinity is Plato's tripartite theory of the soul, and his dialogs taught imperial powers how to rule over man's divine nature. Right down to the names of those sacrificed beside Jesus is also a spiritual allegory that I found even within myself. In all this, I see God in man that is self-governed, and within the story of the crucifixion is man's divine nature.

This is what I see in the meaning of the two men crucified beside Jesus. Dismas, "to the west," and my perception sunset and Gestas, "to moan or complain," our ego and the I am/Jesus our divine thought. It's spiritual alchemy, with sun in man that rises from within. This encouraged the spiritual death in man, making the sun in man set. I see it as a clever spiritual trap where man was led by his lower nature. This belief fed our ego and reassurance that we ourselves collectively taught. Unless you were a gnostic Christian.

Romans 6:3–4 says, "Or do you not know that so many of us as were baptized into Christ Jesus were baptized into his death? Therefore we are buried with him through baptism into death, that just as Christ was raised up from the dead by the glory of the Father, even so we also should walk in newness of life" (New King James Version).

Sometimes I feel like the flawed character Brian from the Monty Python movie *Life of Brian*: "You don't need to follow anybody! You've got to think for yourselves." Like Brian writing on the wall, and the Roman guard screwing with him by correcting him for his terrible grammar. That is my experience from the beginning of sharing my thoughts online. As flawed as I am with my grammar and rhetoric, I see the common person equally flawed.

As I learned all this history, I have become increasingly aware of the world of awakened minds. I am sharing nothing new, and my experience is a spiritual truth to those who know themselves. All the answers to life's tough questions are right before us, but so many of us are blinded by our self-truths. This for me has been my calling and ignited my purpose to be a light in this spiritual darkness, in this dream world.

Romans 3:4 says, "God refused to allow: yes, let God be true, but every man a liar; as it is written, that your power be justified in the sayings, and overcome when judged." This theology is "God logic." It is our psychology giving both answers of the just man and the just less at the same time. This perception changes when a man or woman finds his or her divine nature from within. For those of you reading this who haven't yet experienced this life force, you are the ones in the dark parroting what you have heard.

Plato's tripartite theory is the formula I see for man to reach God. This is the unity of God in man that I put together. Remember, I am human, and I am flawed but I want this to get out there! Tri-unity/trinity God but first your soul/psyche needs to be self-governed. Take the trinity, side by side with the tripartite theory. Father is logic and son is appetitive and the holy spirit is spirited. They created a myth to conceal the function of the God in man. This is a battle the gnostic Christians fought with the exoteric side of Christianity that is government/imperial control.

3

---

[3] These three parts of the psyche also correspond to the three classes of society. Whether in a city or an individual, justice is declared to be a state of the whole in which each part fulfills its function of the appetitive 'carnal desire' is to produce and seek pleasure. The function of the logic is to gently rule through the love of learning. The function of the spirited is to obey the direction from the logic while ferociously defending the

Therefore I say trinity is tripartite in trivium. The trinity is the three roads that lead to God. The tripartite theory is the three roads that lead to a self-governed soul. Finally, is the three roads that lead to truth, the trivium, grammar, logic, and rhetoric. It is also my acronym for the three T.T.T. on the cover of this book. Trinity is tripartite in trivium the god soul truth, T.T.T.

---

whole, often taking the specific form in which the spirited listens instead to the appetitive, while they together either ignore the logical entirely or employ it in the pursuits of pleasure. (Plato's republic)

# 7

Throughout this experience of God in mind, I wanted to share my truth. So many questions and so much history to go through. I realize most people don't really want to know and are happy living with a lie. From what I have learned, most people don't want to face their fears, let alone have their reality shattered. I am not for that person, I am for those who want to evolve to a higher state of consciousness, who, like myself, want a better world!

I question the intentions of our world leaders and imperial families. I think they lost their way in thought and became one giant corporate rule. I can't imagine anyone who has reached his or her higher self ever wanting to cause harm, unless these people are at war with themselves. No matter. I see it is all for the greater good/commonwealth/new world order and the recreation of the god soul with intelligence. Understanding government using religion and its relationship to philosophy shows good intension. Within 12 apostle names I found this!

"This is confirmed by what happens in states; for legislations make the citizens good by forming habits in them, and this is the wish of every legislature, and those who do not effect it miss their mark, and it is this that a good constitution differs from a bad one."[4]

There are great messages throughout the Bible that I can't deny are an inspiration of an innate god of thought that the scribes fused in the mythologies using philosophy. It doesn't matter to me what the world believes. I know what is believed, without question, is willful ignorance. We've been trained to follow and not question for ourselves and that should not be. Not all souls have good intensions. There has always been political evil and the love of money.

The world is complex, and the imperial powers took the bait from the great philosophers and incorporated their thought into their divine rulings. "Kings are justly called gods for that they exercise a manner or resemblance of

---

[4] Aristotle, Nicomachean Ethics, Book 2.

divine power upon earth."[5] This is one of many unjust examples of unjust rulers claiming to be something they are not. Yet his Bible holds authority to so many minds and his claim as God, like all the other unjust gods written in the good book. Saint Constantine the Great, one of many imperial rulers that became deified, was important and responsible for changing from the Serapis faith to the perception of today's Christianity. Arius of Alexandria fought to clarify the government religion of Serapis to be a false god. If you look at Roman coins during this time, you will find the beheaded Serapis with Arius. Using Plato's tripartite theory, they created their apologies for their physical version of Christ, which was Caesar.

---

[5] James VI and I (1610). A Speech to the Lords and Commons of the Parliament at White-Hall.

This is why I see our true timeline is Byzantine Caesar AD. I do not agree with the perception of the Christ by Christian historians. It is an activation of your spiritual connection and not a man. Following the money will tell a different story. This pagan is the first Christian to receive divine messages from the sun god, Apollo. The meaning of Christ even in those days meant something completely different. It's a game of telephone, and our divine connection can't get through because of the story we believe.

Yes, this is my perception, and there are many who see the invention of Jesus and have written about it. I am not saying there isn't a divine source. I am saying we attached a story to it, and it's political evil and very much imperial rule over our divine nature. There are so many apologies for the defense of the physical Christ for the unquestioned minds that are spiritually blinded by myths.

No amount of history is going to sway the believer to the perception I hold. The only way I seen this was through my spiritual experiences. I know history lies, and men ruled by their lower nature is arrogance. Our higher self will not compete with self-truth. This is something that is not seen when our minds are unjust and ruled by an outside source of collective rhetoric, claiming truth.

Even our world map is laid out by ruling empires through colonization. They did this with the authority of their perception of God and their systems of education and law. I will admit that this advanced the world in one way and set us back spiritually. It's a great big game, and our ignorance and greed are a great motivator for the imperial regimes turning corporate. Their way of rule advances while hiding behind the corporate veil. Most of us are just trying to get by in life.

I even see the United States and every country granted independence by the Holy Roman Emperor starting with King George III, a brilliant creation by appearing to lose. The Declaration of Independence is an imperial creation to get conquered territories to rule themselves with the education that was given to them. When I see the United States and its rhetoric by creating statist in a Roman way. I know King George was a brilliant political mind and created a republic that was a mix of Roman, Greek, and Alexandrian, a true Platonist. Our founding fathers knew this, just look at Washington D.C. You have to know history to know our country through its architecture and naming of states. It all ties in together with imperial rule and our divine nature. Just look at our first free mason George Washington and the museum in Alexandria Virginia. Nothing is hidden and it's all right under our noses.

Only someone with a kingly education and the power of world trade, connected by blood to world imperial families, could pull off a creation like this. I think if we could read his letters without the royal family's control on what wasn't released, we would see a very different King George and him playing both sides in his creation. Our ignorance of all this was created by corporations and for good reason. Money! Today, ignorance is our choice and our will to know what we truly are is our own will. Take advantage of it! Trinity is tripartite in trivium the god soul truth.

# 8

Ruled by the "Pinky and the Brain" mentality, we are the evil geniuses marching fourth in our self-destructive nature. Today, in our crown chakra pandemic, the universe has a funny way of showing our mirrored insanity. It really is up to us what we believe. I often wonder, is it really a bad thing if we destroy our world and humanity ends? Maybe this is how we would free our cosmic energy that is playing in this sun god show of doom and gloom.

As dumb as some of us are, there are some really brilliant minds out there. I think many are out there who understand the quantum physics level of our life force and are trying to tap into this free energy. I also get the notion that whatever new science breakthrough there is, it's most likely much older, and the unjust side of man had found ways to capitalize while getting closer to this self-destructive goal. I think we overlook the whistle blowers and call them conspiracy theorists. In our Pinky way, we help the unjust Brain out of sheer ignorance.

Everything from the CERN particle collider (aka God particle collider) that was claimed to be misinformation to the light-based quantum computing super computer, we are advancing in our sciences and can enter the dream state of our consciousness. We have the technology to invade the soul of our electromagnetic energy. We know to enter through our delta, theta, alpha, and beta waves. These energy waves are not products of the brain. It is our life-force energy. That is my self-truth: universes and not science. But Science can be bias just like history. It's only as good as the people governing it.

Our technologies are advancing so rapidly at the helm of corporate political evil. At this point, religion doesn't even matter. The unjust-minded can tap into our biology and affect our mental state as well as our health. This spiritual battle has become something that is a true will to overcome. The lower nature of man will be controlled by these outside forces. They are creating flesh robots out of humans. This is why it is so important to question our self-truths.

Most of us are being programed by the lower god and not the higher self. This is a division!

So my awakening of my mind's eye has certainly created the ultimate conspiracy theorist. I am aware you can find anything to support a view and it takes logic and reasoning to prevail. I choose not to be panicked by this, and I just want others to look into all I have written. It would be tough to prove anything, and this is certainly my personal experience and not anyone else's.

At the beginning of this wild experience I received a warning. I feel this is the perfect place to put this. This message is about seven years old and very disturbing because this was shown through my mind. I wrote the experience down and have shared it before. Our higher self is seeing everything playing out with no one to tell. Yes, I am saying this spiritual nature is relying on us for this inner connection. We have to choose, and that is how we are chosen. This came to me in a heavy vibrating state of energy, and I was very connected to Source when this experience took place. It came like a dream at night because the body and mind has to be at rest. The paragraph below is my stream of consciousness, my dream.

For those who are developing ear-piercing death through tone. Stop! Turn around before destiny is met. Our minds are all interconnected and I am you. You, I, me are everywhere, and you will end you. There is a man who knows the plan. Remember! I am you! Again we will never stand! I have seen you take the uncut money from the women sitting down, and she was unguarded. There was something funny said. In a dream, I showed three lay dead in a room full of technology. Seen through a fourth victims head, felt unbearable brain pain ear-piercing scream death unfavorable!...

"You offspring universe, infinite mind, genius offspring development" and this is the acronym I was taught: You, I'm God! Our consciousness the energy within is god.

It is a mind-universe-system-enlightenment, our muse. This is done through everything and everyone, and in our music is the perception/filter mind of the higher and lower nature of what we are. If you listen and look behind the words, a common narrative is sung throughout the world. God has always been in and out of existence but held prisoner by unjust beliefs.

Why doesn't this intelligence just fix what is wrong? It's the free will of each part of this endless energy that is this selfless God in mind. This duality of this negative and positive energy is psychologically driven and is divided by thought. We are creating our minds through existence, and if we destroy our world, we destroy the opportunity for the birth of new human thought and the experience of training the mind in existence. How else can a being be human? That is, to be!

It's a polarity state in consciousness that I have experienced. This is why we need to be self-governed in thought and to connect to something greater. I think there is a uniqueness to this earth and existence to our souls. I know we are a star phenomenon intergraded and released in time. The spirit is a collective and independent experience. Our world is the ultimate stage, playing out for all this universe life to thrive in the physical realm of possibilities.

Please! I urge everyone to fix their own minds, the key to you is within, get aligned! It is time to come together and prevail within our innate intelligence. Trinity is tripartite in trivium the god soul truth.

# 9

My death and resurrection is part of my spiritual alchemy and self-discovery of the "hidden gold" within (Plato). Everyone has this ability to let the inner genius prevail and become self-anointed. This, like all spiritual awakenings, is self-evident and is a self-governed activation of mind in truth of self. Before my experience, I would have laughed at this notion. This truth is written all throughout the ancient world. Only when you experience the eye of truth from within can you know it.

This process happened gradually for me, and it's good thing. If it happened all at once, I might have gone insane from the experience or tormented those around me and ended up in a straitjacket. The higher universe is kind and gentle in its ways. The lower nature of universe is not, and that's the spiritual part of the awakening of the mind that terrorizes the soul. Until realized, when you attract and address it, then belief can rule unjustly on the spiritual side as well. This is not for the weak-minded, and fear can distract you from truth. This is a fate we may all meet at the end of existence.

I have experienced so much from the flow of energy through me, my chakras illuminating all the way to the crown chakra. The crown chakra can be seen through your spiritual eye and is self-evident. Even the eye of God is seen through this transformation. A deep blue eye, what an amazing experience! I experienced seeing seven rays of light spike out from my head. Just like the Statue of Liberty or Apollo standing on the temple of Artemis, a perfect example of a sun god.

I also experienced a drawing in of my energy that revealed my nonbeing state. As I look back at my notes on this experience, this happened after a second download of the black shadow moving across my inner vision. I wrote that I remembered looking at the clock at 3:33 a.m. I was lying in bed resting in a fetal position toward my wife. I was trying to sleep but heard a buzzing sound. Tones, buzzing, and humming are a big part of this. Awareness of other energies is part of the awakening, and we are not alone.

The sound I heard all night was increasing in volume, and I felt fast vibrations throughout my body. My head was humming. My own tinnitus picked up and flowed in unison with this energy. It suddenly spiked to a deafening ringing. At this point, if someone tried to speak to me, there is no way I could hear anything or anyone. When the tone spiked, so did the vibrations I was experiencing. I felt my energy retract into my body, and I became very small. At that instant I realized what I thought was me wasn't me at all.

I was the size of a pea and was vibrating very fast. I could see completely around the sphere I am. I was pure energy, and my thoughts and fears were intact. This scared the shit out of me! Suddenly I found myself in the cave of my mouth, just behind my tonsils.

I could see perfectly, and I was a blue light in this state of nonbeing. Even though I was an orb of light, I still felt my energy retract from my face and feel it harden as my mouth opened up. I was frozen in fear sitting there in amazement of what death actually is. I was not ready to go! I was completely alone but I felt a presence. I could hear my inner voice beyond the ringing energy of my soul.

I begged God not to let me go! I didn't want to leave my family! Here I was thinking this is the end, and as fast as this experience took place, my energy expanded back to my body. I immediately looked over at the clock. It read 5:03 a.m. The amount of time that this took place felt like thirty seconds, but ninety minutes had gone by. This could have been a dream, but life is often referred to as a dream.

I have also experienced picking up radio signals in my head. What I have learned is that our pineal gland is a spiritual receiver and transmitter of thought. Not only can we reconnect to our greater thought, we have the ability to connect to each other. This is why I am not so concerned about this book changing the world. All we need we possess from within ourselves. We are all interconnected and only divided by thought. When we silence the mind of unjust thought, the universe will open up to you, and the power of true intention will take place.

Numbers certainly play a big part in this. I am guided by them and they are a reminder of my intentions. They show me how connected everything is, and I am aware that I don't always understand the meaning. The synchronicities of my daily life is a constant reminder that there is a greater truth to be rediscovered. I use it to learn and find truth. When in line with this cosmic perspective, the numbers that reach my soul pop up in my life. I followed my numbers in learning world history and my purpose to find truth in this world of illusions.

Plato covered all this as well as Aristotle and I think we need to look deeper within their writings. Before my experience, I couldn't tell you anything about Plato or Aristotle. When you become awakened to this phenomenon of mind. Metaphysical thought will carry more weight in your thought on how to evolve. I think it is time to take thought seriously because our nature needs this to go beyond this physical reality. Keep in mind, world truth is twisted and is consistently changing all the time. What we consider good sources for truth, can be manipulated. Therefore, I see we need to go within and awaken ourselves to our divine nature. You cannot trust the world and its manipulated history and science. Trinity is tripartite in trivium, the god soul truth.

# 10

I think about the people throughout my life and what I have learned. We all appear to be suffering from something. So many people live in reaction to what is believed. It really does come down to self-accountability to our thoughts and reactions. To believe in something outside yourself in order to save yourself from your hellish thought is to live a lie. It's all about self-mastery, and our goal to reach our divine nature from within. This is the battle we all are in, and our unquestioned mind is ruled by our lower ego. Don't you think you should have the keys to your eternal mind?

I don't have all figured out, but I am willing to open my heart and mind to this higher nature of truth in consciousness. My children are teaching me that I have more to learn because I still find myself unjust in the way I govern them. Children will certainly test you. I think a lot about my experience as a child, and now I understand why we parents are so mean to our children: we ourselves are children of mind and haven't evolved in our way of being. It is so important to question our own minds because this is our heaven or hell on earth or in heaven.

My self-truth is subjective, like all self-truths, but I see a universal truth of God in mind. Like all the great spiritual philosophies that are echoed throughout the past and present, whether parroted by believers or lived through those in the knowing, this is our free will to make the connection or be enslaved by beliefs. This life we live can be a hell or a heaven, and I am hopeful that the key to heaven can open our hearts, and the key to hell is to observe and never forget but to forgive.

Through my own chaotic mind I have prevailed against my own vicious nature, but sometimes it still visits. I am aware of it and do my best to not feed it. I have learned to sit in the silence of my mind to make the connection and to not trust every thought I encounter; just sit with it and question it. I have learned to feel the energy that flows from within and be in the moment when I am in that meditative state of awareness.

I learned God can be liar with condemning and evil narcissistic love. I also know God can be the genius to my intellect and is my personal savoir to my throne of God though my pineal gland. To experience the sunrise from within and illumination of my very being is to know I have everything I need to live eternally. This life is a contradiction and conundrum of thought in soul. The only place I can find God is within a self-governed soul.

I only wanted peace of mind when I discovered my own divinity. In all that I had learned, I wanted to share and be the example for others to silence self-hate. We all wear that crown of thorns and drag that heavy cross when ruled by our unjust ego mind. I think we should lay it down and learn to not be martyrs. I am tired of the same old story of sacrifice for the world. Do it yourself! Sacrifice your own hellish thought. Haven't we paid enough for belief? I want to see the true liberation of God in self. Not some knockoff government creation that nobody could live up to. We are human and perfectly flawed and there is so much more. I just want this crown chakra pandemic of God trapped by ego mind to end. I want to see truly awakened minds, not parroting self-condemning believers. It is time to know in God! This is my divine message from the great I am that rose through myself and is my truth.

It is easier to sway a point of view through confusion, fear, and hate than to live with love and not dominate. The open mind can receive infinite wisdom. The narrow mind is small and a personal prison. To live with love is to rise above. To live with hate is to commiserate. To live with fear, nothing is clear. This will only drive you apart. Come on, people! Don't you think you are smart? I am everyone, I have learned to be. Without confusion, fear, and hate, I have learned to see. In all this I have learned to question my self-truths and learned to be true. Go ahead and drop the ego, it will only make a monkey out of you.

The grass is greener on this side of the mind, with open fields and mountains I can climb. It truly is exciting to live with something new! I didn't have to go anywhere, it is all inside you. Just like a eureka moment, I should have known all along. We have been given the wrong address, and this is how we get it wrong. We have confused the word of God with confusion, fear, and hate. Just remember, love never discriminates.

I put my trust in "Jesus I am," the selfless man. To know God's love and selfless plan. I was mad at you for teaching me to be me. But now I know what sets me free. Confusion, fear, and hate was the lesson. The thought that counts is love and only from within, so say hello to heaven.

This is my will for truth to be known. This life we live can seem uncertain in all its confusion, fear, and hate. These are my answers to this life and the path we walk alone and together through thought. The body is only training for the mind to know existence. Be mindful, and may God prevail in you. Question those self-truths because that is your prison.

Trinity is tripartite in trivium, the god soul truth, **T.T.T.**

Printed in the United States
by Baker & Taylor Publisher Services